A FIELD GUIDE
TO THE BIRDS
OF WESLEYAN

To Rich Stallcup
1944–2012

The Pirate
of Point Reyes

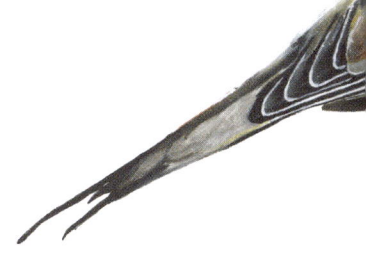

A FIELD GUIDE
TO THE BIRDS
OF WESLEYAN

*Written and Illustrated
by Oliver James*

Wesleyan University Press
Middletown, Connecticut

Wesleyan University Press
Middletown CT 06459
www.wesleyan.edu/wespress

A Field Guide to the Birds of Wesleyan was
published by Stethoscope Press, Wesleyan
University, in Spring 2014 in a limited edition of
300 copies. The first Wesleyan University Press
edition was published in Fall 2014.

Manufactured in the United States of America.

ISBN 978-0-8195-7563-0 (pbk)

5 4 3 2 1

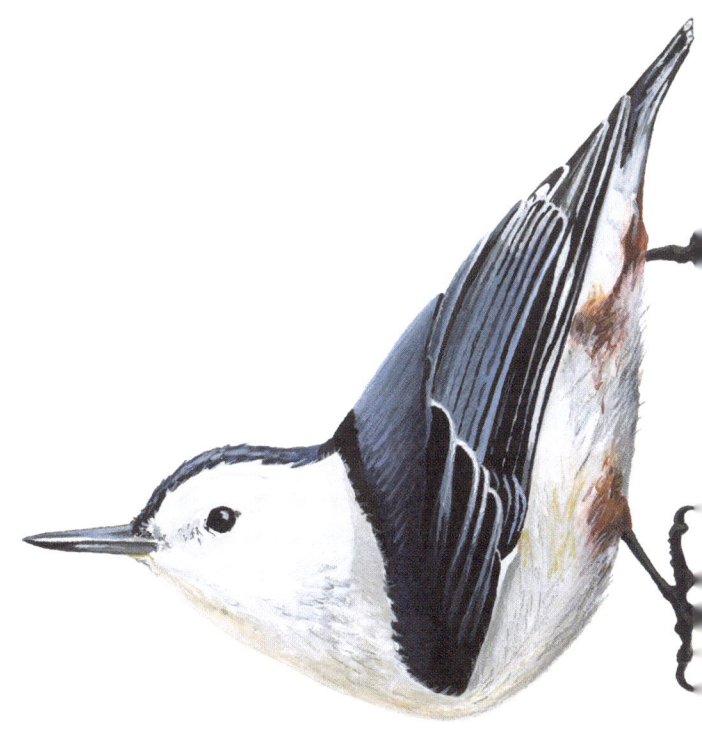

TABLE OF
CONTENTS

AUTHOR'S NOTE

The inspiration for this field guide arose while co-leading a student forum in the spring of 2013 titled "An Introduction to Field Ornithology and the Birds of Central Connecticut." During my time at Wesleyan there were no courses offered in the Biology Dept. that were predominately field-based. I organized the forum out of a desire to fill this gap, to introduce students to the rewards of natural history and unearth the potential for learning biology and ecology beyond the confines of the textbook and the lab. In this way, my motivations were twofold: to de-intellectualize and to inspire. Moving forward, my generation will need everything it can muster. As I sit here at my desk at 124 High St., the world has just closed out one of the most extreme climatic years in recorded history. Ecological change is occurring rapidly. The answers that we need to navigate this perilous time will only come from close observation and a collective ecological acumen. The prerequisites for this kind of knowledge don't include a PhD or a lab to analyze ice cores from Antarctica. Birds, for one, are excellent indicators of environmental change. *Birds are found everywhere*. And yet, one of the most common reactions I receive when sharing stories about encounters with birds is surprise over the sheer diversity and quantity of birds that surround us, immediately. This reaction, I believe, betrays a symptom unique to a generation born into a shrinking world. It is a byproduct of the pervasive clarion call of the day: the world is bruised. A bruised world is a small world. As humans proliferate, non-human animals are squeezed into smaller and smaller spaces. It is not surprising, then, that today biodiversity is often conceptualized to be elsewhere, remote, somewhere you need a plane ticket and a guide to get to; it is certainly not right here, at school, at work, at home. This book hopes to correct this misconception, to bring it home, to crack open the drama and magic of the world that has since eluded our attention.

Our world is smaller, but not that small. In other words, nature is resilient. Today's eco-consciousness reminds us of the sobering fact that there no longer exists a place on the planet that has escaped the ecological mark of humanity. This, perhaps, is a critical bulletin necessary to inculcate us with a sense of scale, of restraint and of action. Read another way, it would seem as if we were the only species ever to have shaped the organization of the world. Our anthropocentrism is alive and well. Meanwhile, we humans, whether we are aware of it or not, brush shoulders every day with creatures who continue to navigate the planet in ancient, complex ways. There is a vast, mysterious, and immensely rewarding world whirring along parallel to ours right under our noses. It is right there, bruised as it may be. *Right here*. There is magic and high drama occurring every day in your own backyard. It is just a matter of learning again how to see it.

OLIVER JAMES

Middletown, CT
January, 2014

INTRODUCTION

This field guide is designed for a specific audience: the students, faculty, and staff that live, study, and work at Wesleyan University. Described in the following pages are 16 of the most common birds to Wesleyan's campus. Although the book should simultaneously be useful as an introduction to the birds of Middletown, CT, that is not the express intention of this guide. This book pertains specifically to the birds regularly found on Wesleyan campus grounds, and excludes such nearby features as the Connecticut River. The choice to feature these specific 16 species over others remains, of course, a subjective decision. This guide should not be confused as definitive, statistically speaking. There are a host of other species that regularly frequent the area that can be located without much effort. More accurately, this book features the 16 most expected species drawn from the personal observations of the author over a four-year undergraduate residence (2010 – 2014). These observations were passive by nature: they consist largely of the observations accumulated during the harried daily circuit of a student. It is important to note as well that as climate and habitat changes, both regionally and on campus, so too will bird populations change.

PRESENTATION AND ORGANIZATION

This book features original color illustrations of each species in mixed media (watercolor, gouache, and colored pencil). The technical and compositional choices employed in these paintings betray a careful balance between competing goals, namely function and aesthetics. It should be immediately apparent that the compositional choices of these paintings diverge from traditional field guide format. Instead of having each bird presented in profile, so that every feather and field mark may be equally visible, the birds in this guide are presented in many different postures. Each bird is depicted in a way that attempts to capture the beauty and physicality unique to each species while also highlighting the key field marks needed for ready and accurate identification.

As this field guide is directed towards beginning birders, it should be noted that each individual bird in the field (i.e. individuals within a species) will never be identical one to the next. Each bird, depending on its age, sex, subspecies, range, life history, or the time of year of observation, will display contrasting field marks, subtly or strikingly so. For instance, many species (but not all) are sexually dimorphic: plumage, body size and proportion, and behavior differ between the sexes. Furthermore, all species have unique juvenile plumages that often differ dramatically from the adult. Due to constraints of time and space, this field guide does not attempt to feature all of this intraspecific variation.

Instead, each species features one individual that is fairly representative of the population unique to the region. The field marks essential to the identification of this bird are highlighted in the account that accompanies each species. When a species is strongly sexually dimorphic, the opposite sex is also described. Juvenile birds are not described. Vocalizations are briefly described. The remainder, and majority, of the text offers a brief anecdotal depiction of the behavior and personality of the bird. Every species, each individual, has a distinctive way of moving through the world, of interacting with their environment. Not only are these qualities often overlooked as useful field marks, they are the most rewarding aspects of patient wildlife observation, the enchanting performance that deepens the appreciation of common existence between human and animal.

On a final note, the birds in a field guide are typically organized taxonomically; the birds in this field guide are organized in no particular order.

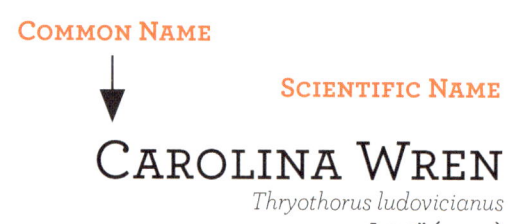

COMMON NAME

SCIENTIFIC NAME

CAROLINA WREN

Thryothorus ludovicianus

L 5.9" (15 cm)

Year Round

SPECIES ACCOUNT

TIME OF YEAR WHEN PRESENT

TOTAL LENGTH (TIP OF BEACK TO TAIL)

Wrens are always busy. A strong eyebrow transfixing its face into a perpetual glare, the Carolina Wren seems to take its work particularly seriously. Instead of constructing just one nest they will often build up to three. This strategy is thought to possibly distract predators from the one active nest. Or perhaps it's the shrewd business design of an ambitious local developer. Wrens forage in dense undergrowth often very close to the ground, meticulously investigating the nooks and crannies inaccessible to most other birds. As they go about their work, their tail is often flipped straight up in the air; the posture seems analogous to the unconscious protrusion of a tongue during intense concentration (à la Michael Jordan). Wrens are also renowned for their breath support. New acquaintances with this little bird are often shocked that such a thunderous sound could possibly emanate from such a small being. Look — and listen — for this species in the backyards along High St. and behind Buddhist House.

IDENTIFICATION: Bold white eyebrow. Whiteish throat. Upperparts reddish brown. Breast and belly buffy-orange.

VOICE: Song is forceful and variable. Most songs consist of short, repeated phrases.

DESCRIPTION OF PRIMARY VOCALIZATIONS

DESCRIPTION OF ESSENTIAL FIELDMARKS

It is useful to have a specific, common vocabulary to describe the parts of a bird when sorting out identification. Following is a template that delineates the feather groups and parts of a bird that are referred to in this guide:

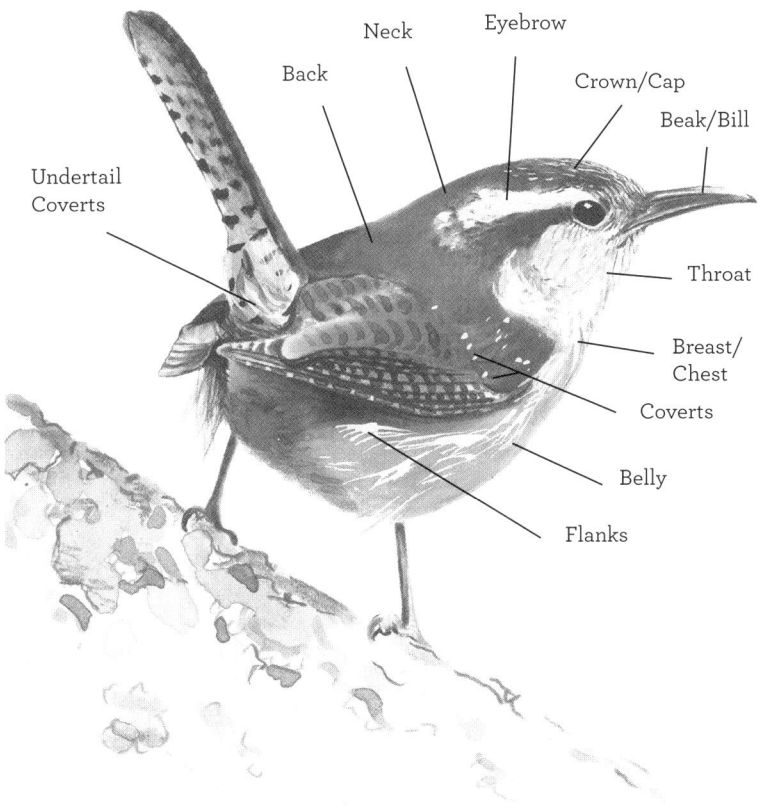

GLOSSARY

Sexually Dimorphic: Phenotypic difference between males and females of the same species.

Song vs. Call: In lay terms, bird songs are the vocalizations made by birds that are diagnostically melodious. Typically, calls are briefer, more simple musically, and not broadcasted in the same manner. Scientifically, calls and songs are differentiated by function. Songs are used to attract mates and declare territorial boundaries. Calls can convey information about relative location in a group and presence of food or danger. Typically, birds can have many calls but have one primary song. Birds, like humans, also have discernible dialects.

A NOTE ABOUT EQUIPMENT

Birds can be shy and elusive even around the most patient observer. Investing in a good pair of binoculars can make a world of difference in easing identification and bringing the nuanced field marks subtle and body language of a bird to life. Too often beginning birders will struggle with poor (or no) optics and grow frustrated at learning the ropes. If you are serious about wildlife observation, consider investing in a decent pair of binoculars.

PLATES

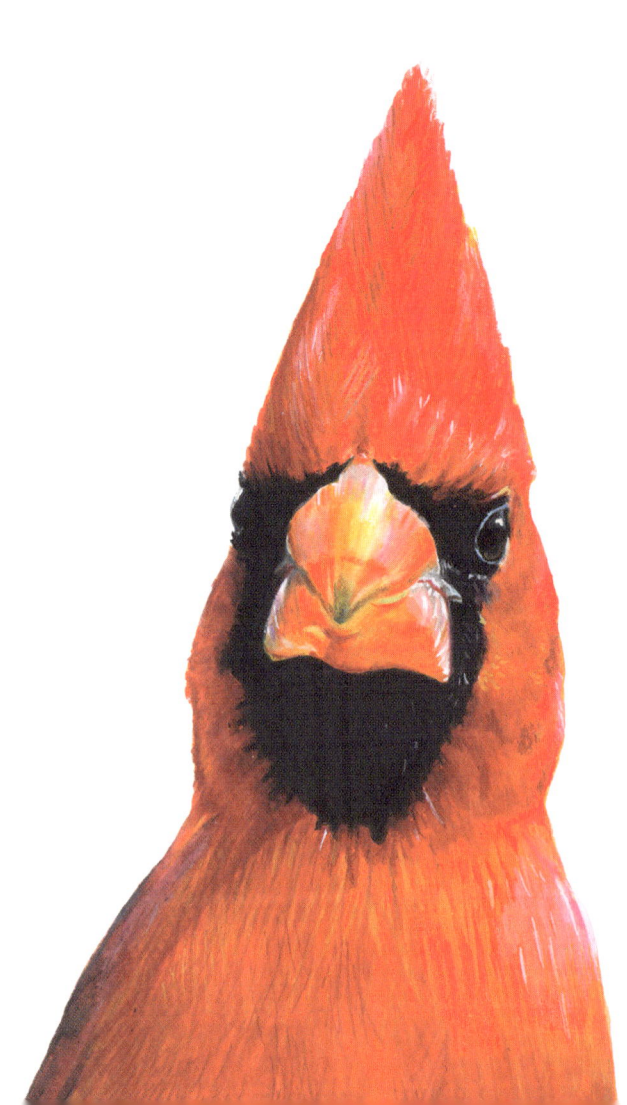

NORTHERN CARDINAL

Cardinalis cardinalis
L 8.7" (22 cm)
Year Round

Sporting its conspicuous red crest, the eponymous Northern Cardinal can be found year round on sweatshirts and coffee mugs across campus. In addition to the homecoming football game, the species is also commonly attracted to suburban feeders where it uses its powerful, conical bill specialized to crush seeds. The Northern Cardinal is arguably one of the most recognizable birds in North America. Its brilliant crimson outfit is arresting. Such gaudy attire is usually ascribed to the ostentatious species of the tropics. Sexually dimorphic, the female retains the crest and overall shape of the male but is buffy-brown overall. Incongruous with his garb, the male is often reticent and will sing from dense foliage. Look for flashes of crimson in the hedges along fraternity row, the habitat adjacent to the Cross St. athletic fields, and in the yards along Mt. Vernon Street.

IDENTIFICATION
Male unmistakable — has a bright red body and pointed crest and a black face. Female is buffy-brown with reddish tinge in the wings, tail and crest. Both sexes have a distinct large, red conical bill.

VOICE
Call is a metallic *chip*. Song is variable, but typically a liquid, whistling *purty purty purty* followed directly by three lower notes *cue cue cue.*

WHITE-BREASTED NUTHATCH

Sitta carolinensis
L 5.8" (15 cm)
Year Round

Physical traits are important in identification, but behavior can be just as useful. Nuthatches are a case-in-point: these acrobatic birds forage by weaving meticulous spirals up and down the barrels of branches and tree trunks looking for small invertebrates hiding in the folds of bark. This is a unique approach — a woodpecker takes a similar one but prefers to start at the bottom of the tree and work up. The nuthatch has no particular preference. It is just as comfortable working face first towards the ground. Less gregarious than the other nuthatches, the White-breasted is often found alone, absorbed in its work, incessantly talking aloud to itself much of the time. Look for nuthatches scouring the large beeches in front of college row and in the pines and maples in the CFA.

IDENTIFICATION
Small, compact features. Grey-blue back and white face and underparts. Black cap that extends down the back of the head. The lower belly and undertail coverts are chestnut.

VOICE
Song is a repeated series of nasal notes, *wha-wha-wha*, usually just 2-4 notes but up to a dozen.

4

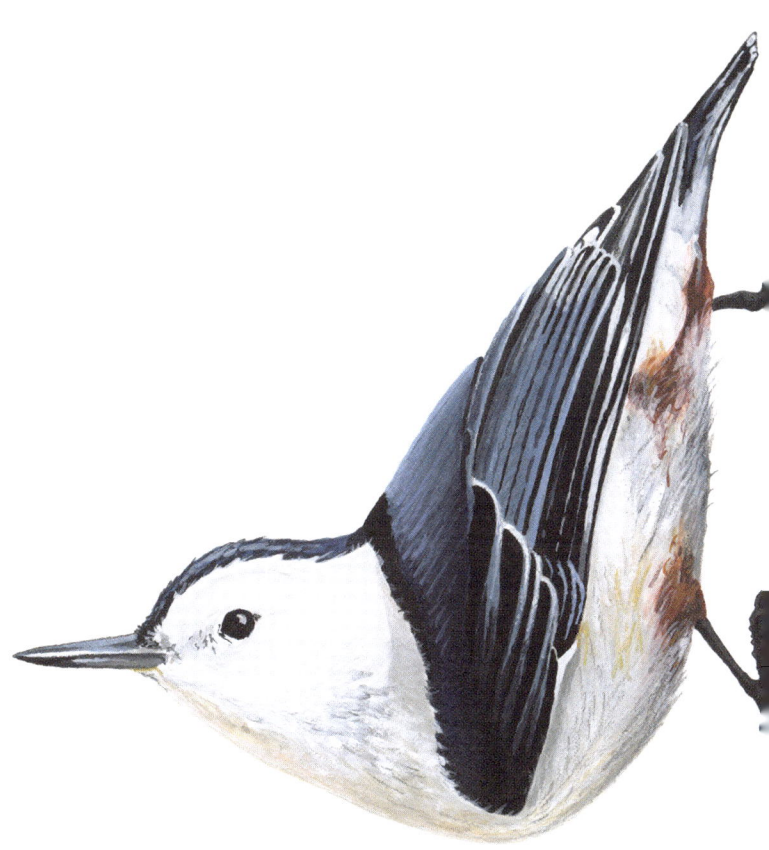

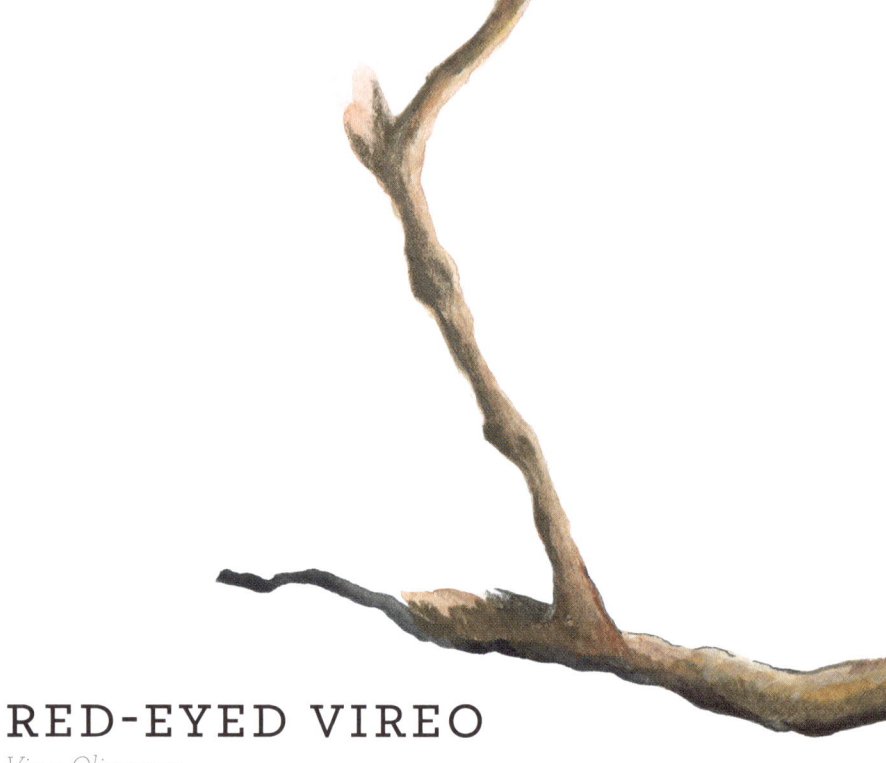

RED-EYED VIREO

Vireo Olivaceus
L 6" (15 cm)
May – August

In the bird world, size is inversely related to exuberance: the smaller you are, the more spunk you radiate. Like many other insectivores, the Red-eyed Vireo seems inexhaustibly ebullient. But there is something unique about the vigor of the Vireo: it is dogged, more akin to the energy of a Border Collie than a Black Lab. This bird brings an intense focus to its musical practice, often singing relentlessly dawn to dusk. They aren't frenetic, however — their body language is more deliberate than most birds of a similar size. Preferring to rehearse from the canopy of the tallest trees around, they can be surprisingly elusive despite their frequent broadcast. Because of their impressive transcontinental itinerary, the Red-eyed Vireo is only on campus for a few weeks of the academic year. They arrive on campus from South America in early May and by mid-August the birds have dispersed and are largely silent. During Senior Week, listen for Red-eyed Vireos in the tall trees in the vicinity of University Relations or Foss Hill.

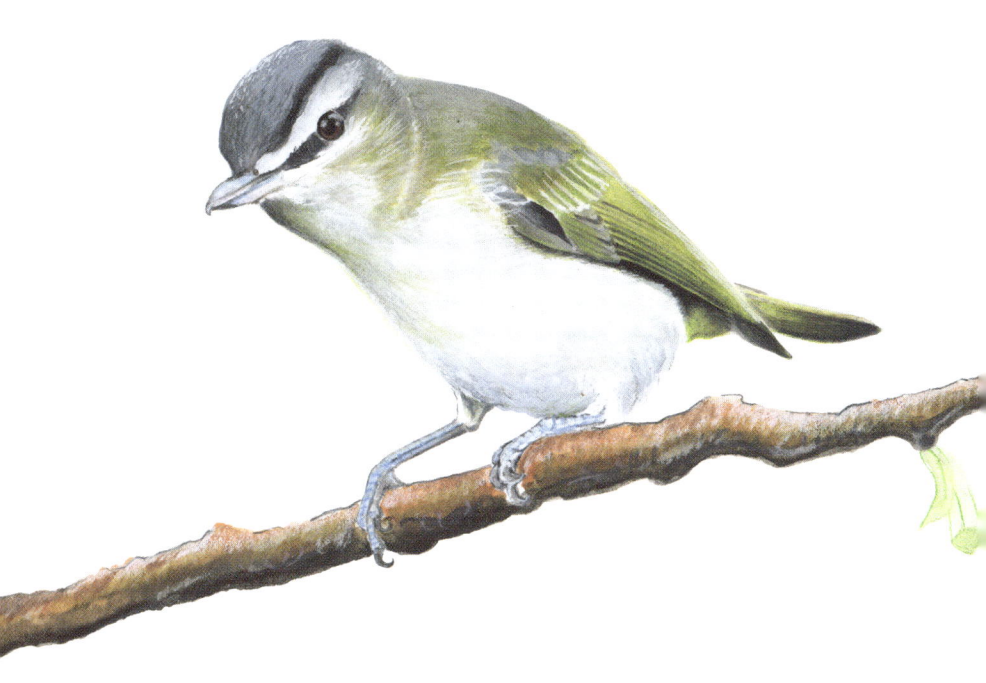

IDENTIFICATION
Bold face pattern: white eyebrow outlined above and below with black. Blue-gray crown contrasts with olive back and wings. Paler underparts.

VOICE
Song is series of short 2-3 note phrases with brief pauses in between. Phrases rise and fall in inflection: *cheer-o-wit, cher-ee, chit-a-wit, de-o*. Call is a scolding, down-slurred *myahh*.

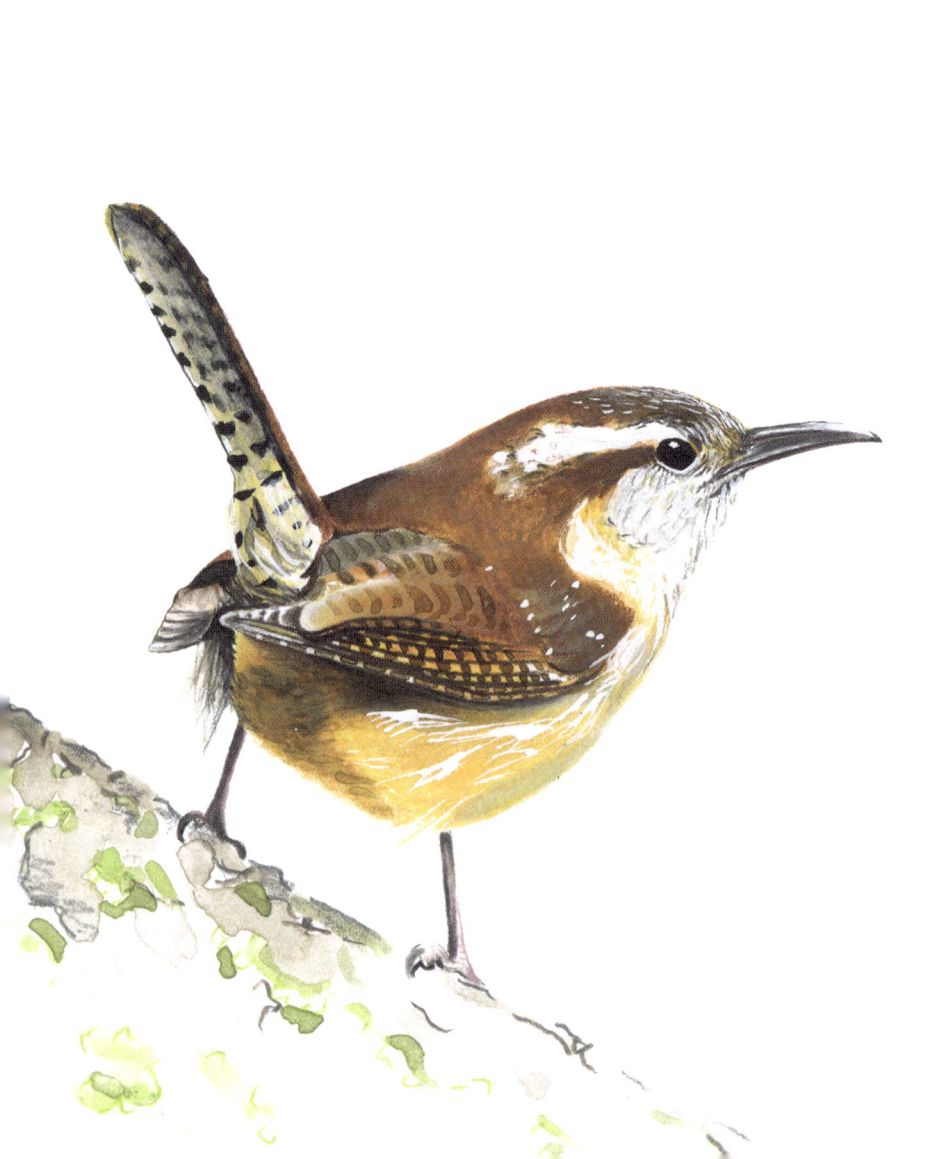

CAROLINA WREN
Thryothorus ludovicianus
L 5.9" (15 cm)
Year Round

Wrens are always busy. A strong eyebrow transfixing its face into a perpetual glare, the Carolina Wren seems to take its work particularly seriously. Instead of constructing just one nest they will often build up to three. This strategy is thought to possibly distract predators from the one active nest. Or perhaps it's the shrewd business design of an ambitious local developer. Wrens forage in dense undergrowth often very close to the ground, meticulously investigating the nooks and crannies inaccessible to most other birds. As they go about their work, their tail is often flipped straight up in the air; the posture seems analogous to the unconscious protrusion of a tongue during intense concentration (à la Michael Jordan). Wrens are also renowned for their breath support. New acquaintances with this little bird are often shocked that such a thunderous sound could possibly emanate from such a small being. Look — and listen — for this species in the backyards along High St. and behind Buddhist House.

IDENTIFICATION
Bold white eyebrow. Whitish throat. Upperparts reddish-brown. Breast and belly buffy-orange.

VOICE
Song is forceful and variable. Most songs consist of short, repeated phrases.

DARK-EYED JUNCO

Junco hyemalis
L 5.9" (15 cm)
Year Round

The Dark-eyed Junco, a type of sparrow, is one of the most wide-ranging birds in North America. Due to its varied distribution, Juncos look very different depending on where you are: in the Southwest they are pinkish-brown but in New England they are charcoal-grey. This variation has lent the bird a turbulent taxonomic history. Until recently the Dark-eyed Junco was split into five distinct species; today it is recognized as one unique species. One day it will likely be split again! A field mark common to all regional flavors of the Junco is the species' white outer tail feathers, which flash discernibly when the birds are flushed. During the winter months, Junco's band together into large groups that forage together for seeds. For a few months out of the year personal space issues can be put aside in favor of the safety that comes in numbers. As you walk around campus during winter, look for staccato bursts of white receding down the path in front of you.

IDENTIFICATION
Charcoal-grey head, breast, back and body. White belly and stout pinkish bill. Outer tail feathers crisp white which contrast against dark central tail feathers in flight.

VOICE
Musical trill that stays at a constant pitch.

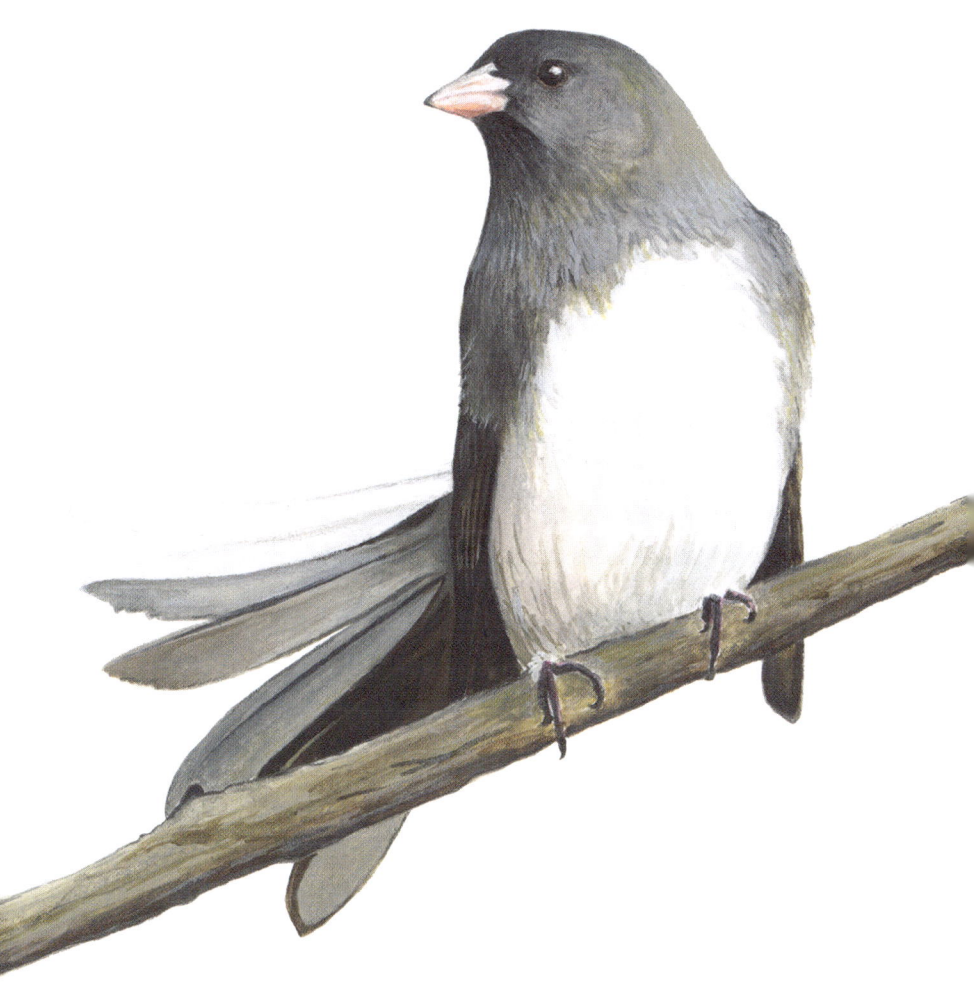

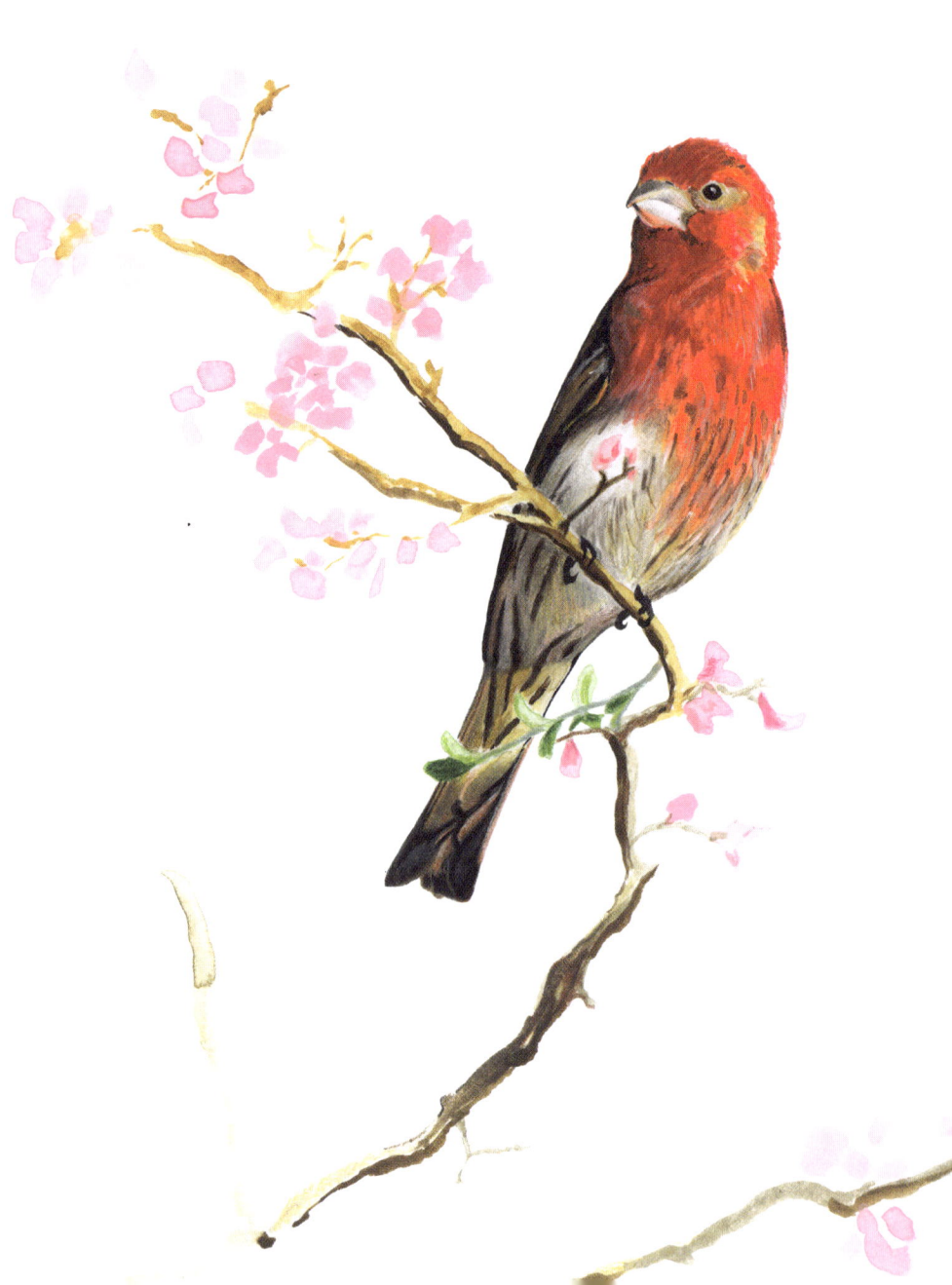

HOUSE FINCH

Carpodacus mexicanus
L 5.3" (15 cm)
Year Round

The House Finch is a relatively recent newcomer to New England. Native to the desert Southwest, a small population was introduced to Long Island in 1940. Within 50 years the population had exploded to every state in the eastern United States. Today, they are a gregarious visitor to feeders, the males recognizable for their cheery red attire. When writing about this bird, what stands out most is how difficult it is to describe its personality. Most other birds in this guide were easy to anthropomorphize — some are argumentative, some are shy. House Finches have a solidly mild demeanor. This is not to say that they are unimpressive. On the contrary, in a world crowded by Type A birds, maybe it's high time to celebrate the beauty of being simply average. Look for House Finches in the big trees along College Row and in the fields along Long Lane.

IDENTIFICATION
The forehead, chest, and rump of the male are strawberry-red. The lower belly and flanks are white with blurry- brown streaks. Female is much drabber. Lacking the red, she is brown overall with heavy, brown streaking.

VOICE
Bright, lively jumble of varied notes and phrases that usually ends in a rising, nasal *wheer.*

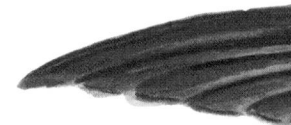

CHIMNEY SWIFT
Chaetura pelagica
L 5.5 " (14 cm)
May – September

Swifts are more bat than bird. Built for ultimate efficiency in the air, their landing gear is too weak to support the body in an upright position. Instead, they roost vertically, clinging to the sides of caves and crevices, much like a bat does, except with their heads facing up instead of the other way around. Their entire day is spent in flight, foraging at a high altitude. In fact, swifts are so partial to the sky that these birds might as well have been born on the wing. Superficially similar to swallows, their flight pattern actually has the same fluttery, sporadic quality of a diurnal bat. Looking up at them from below they have been described as little "cigars with wings," whizzing around incessantly, mouths agape, inhaling airborne insects to their hearts' content. Their vocalizations are even bat-like. With the surge of urbanization and loss of natural habitat over the last century, swirling flocks of Chimney Swifts have become a common sight overhead in cities across the eastern United States. The inside of an idle chimney makes for a perfect protected spot to spend the night. This tenancy gives them their name. Look for Chimney Swifts carving across the sky anywhere above campus.

IDENTIFICATION
Body shape and proportion is unique: long slender wings and small cylindrical body. Brown overall. Fluttery, foraging behavior at high altitudes is unique.

VOICE
Quick, sputtering of notes often run together into a rapid twitter.

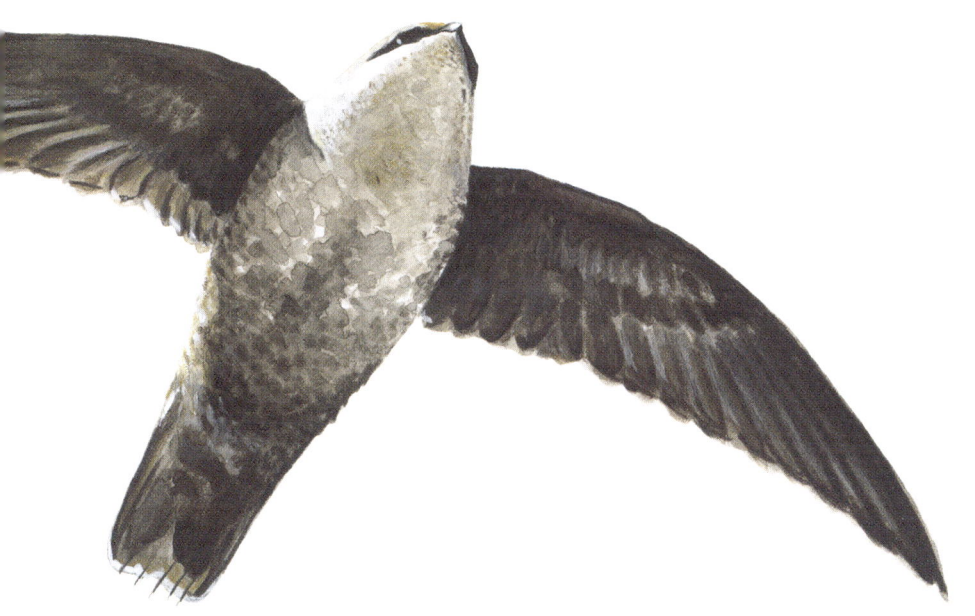

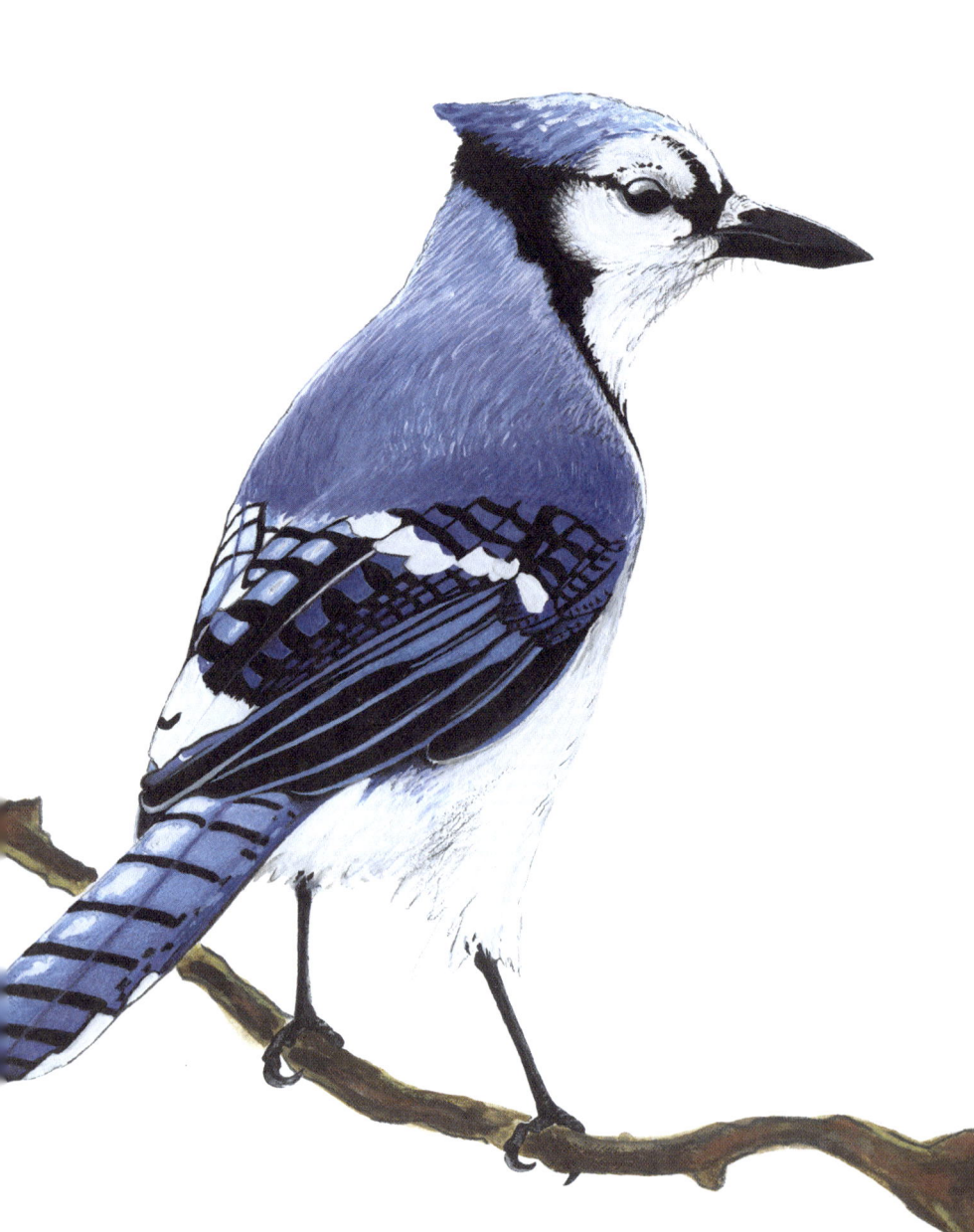

BLUE JAY

Cyanocitta cristata
L 11" (28 cm)
Year Round

Despite being abundantly intelligent, the classroom was never the right habitat for the Blue Jay. These birds have street smarts: this is one of the few species known to have employed tools to secure food rewards in lab experiments. Having dropped out of high school, Blue Jays are truants pursuing cheap thrills. In their favorite version of Russian roulette, the Blue Jay will agitate dangerous birds much larger than they until eliciting a reaction. They also enjoy imitating the screams of birds of prey, getting a kick out of causing neighborhood panic. In addition, jays have a reputation for vandalism, and, not surprisingly, have become a favorite scapegoat for today's social ills. They are misunderstood. Despite occasionally indulging in the eggs of other birds, studies suggest that this destructive behavior is rare. Under-advertised is the fact that Blue Jays, consumers of large quantities of acorns, are thought to have played a critical role in seed dispersal and the expanding range of oaks after the last ice age. What's more, their intimidating cobalt costume is simply a trick of the light. The blue we see is due to the scattering of photons produced by feather structure; if you ground up some of their feathers you'd be left with brown dust. On campus, Blue Jays are often seen shuttling overhead between nearby forest fragments. Look for them as they navigate the airspace over Andrus Field.

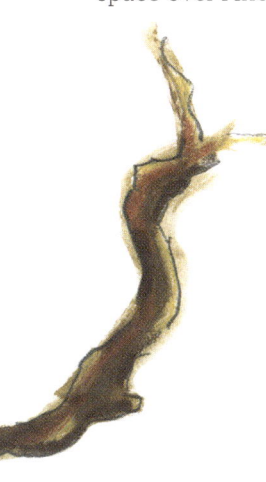

IDENTIFICATION
Unmistakable royal blue crest. White throat bordered with a black "necklace." Blue wings and tail with intricate pattern of black barring and white patches. Underparts are paler.

VOICE
Has a diverse array of vocalizations, often loud and harsh. Can imitate other birds.

TUFTED TITMOUSE

Baeolophus bicolor
L 6.3" (16 cm)
Year Round

Like many other small birds, the decibel level of the Tufted Tit-mouse's music far overcompensates for its small size. Their simple, loud song is given repeatedly, seeming to echo back and forth off the trees. A titmouse is not a self-conscious bird: its opinions are broadcasted assertively, its personal space issues settled noisily. Titmice will often fraternize with their lively relatives, the Chickadees, joining their animated flocks to search the neighborhood for well-stocked feeders. In preparation for the winter, Titmice may stash more than a hundred individual seeds one by one over a small area, returning for them later when food sources are scarce. Fearless of larger beings, this impetuous bird has been known to harvest fur for its nests right off the backs of living animals, including pets. Look for titmice in the backyards on Lawn and Brainerd Avenues.

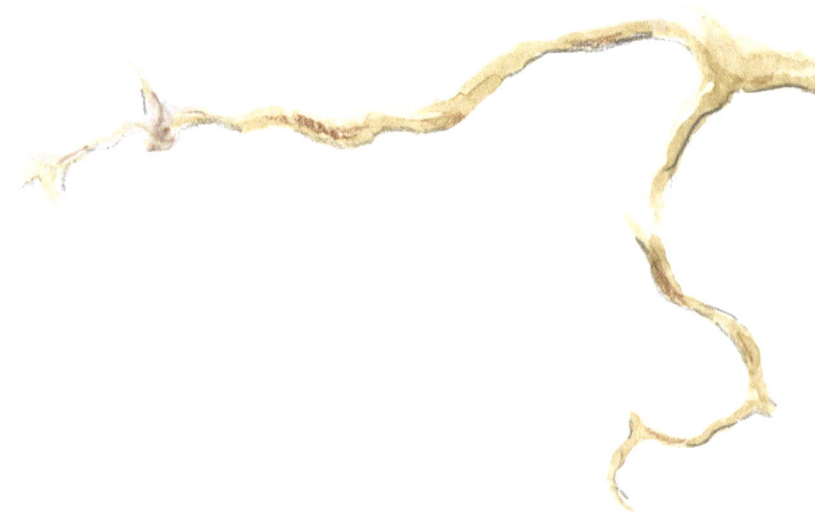

IDENTIFICATION

Gray upperparts, including a short, grey crest. Black forehead. Breast and belly white. Flanks are washed in rusty-orange.

VOICE

Song is a loud, whistled *peter peter peter* often repeated monot-onously.

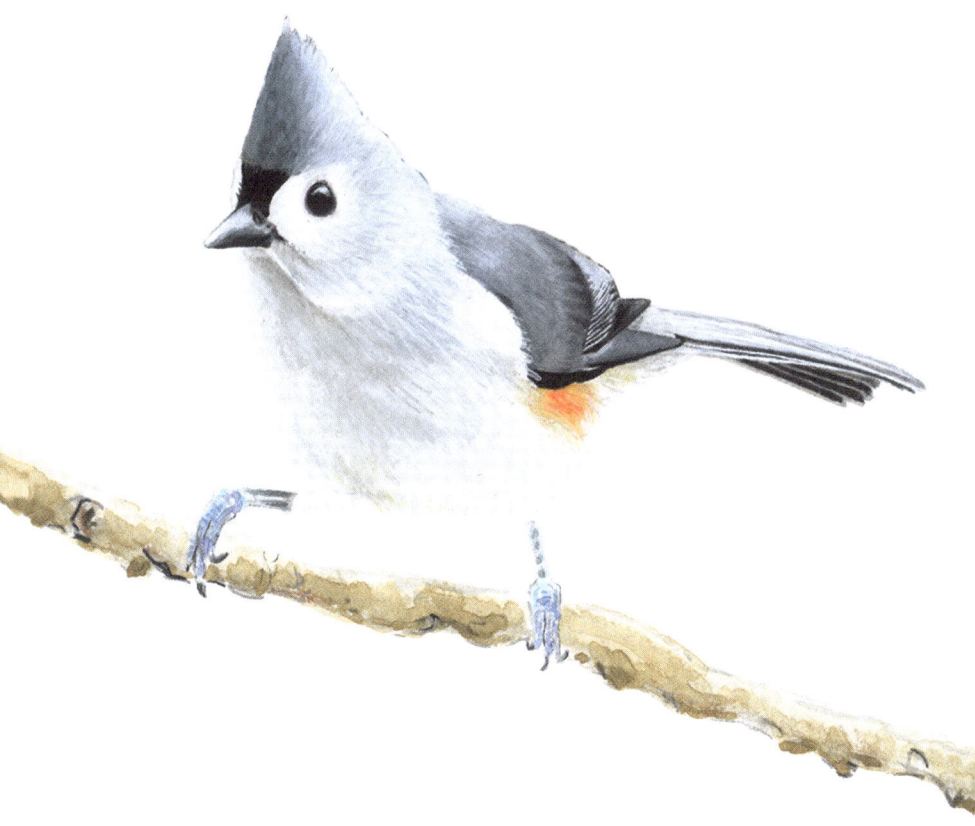

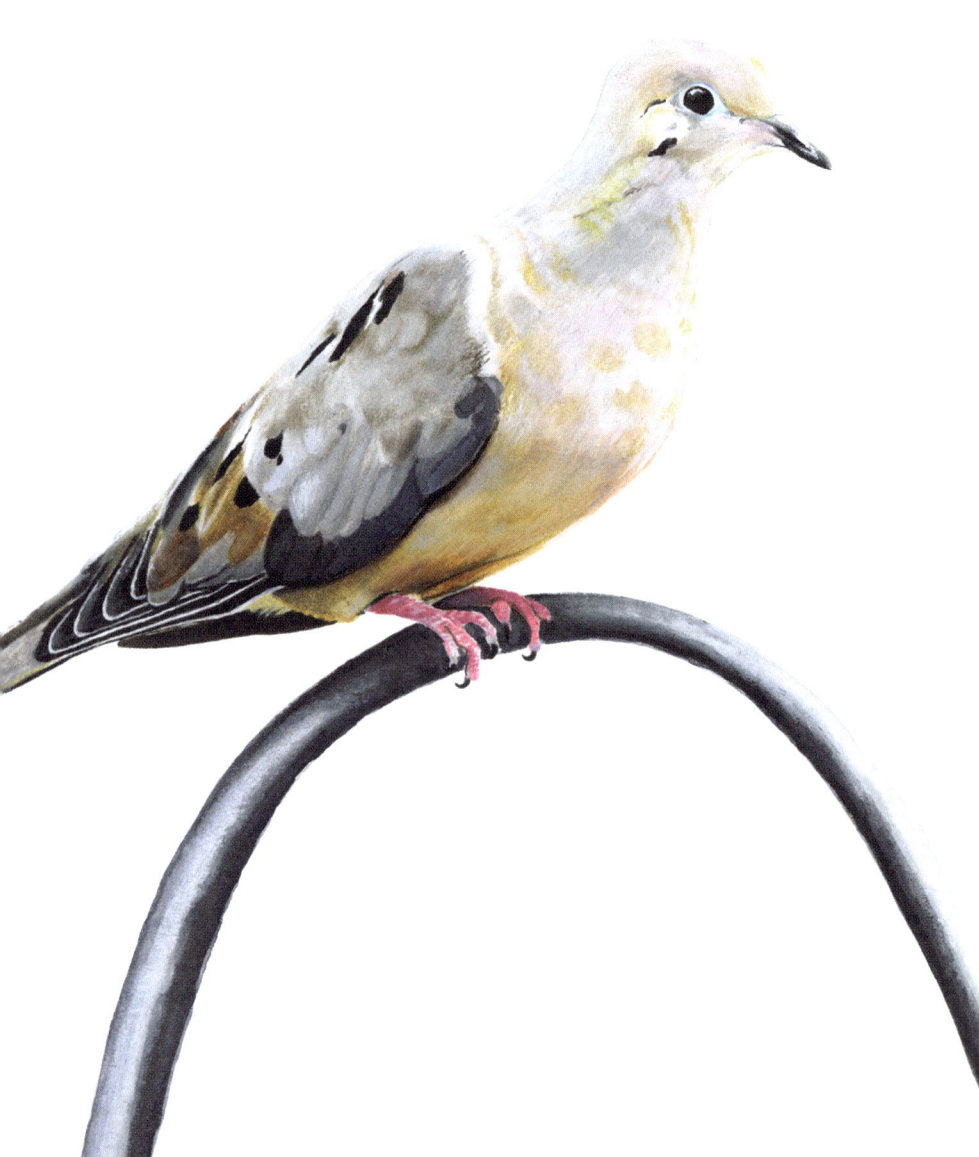

MOURNING DOVE

Zenaida macroura
L 12" (31 cm)
Year Round

Mourning Doves never seem to be completely on the ball. Their ability to think quickly under pressure is lacking and, aside from being able to fly in a straight line very quickly, they have a spatial awareness tantamount to a teenage boy going through puberty. Their small-headed appearance doesn't help to downplay this reputation. But despite not being one of the sharpest tools in the shed, the Mourning Dove is certainly one of the most prolific birds on the continent, able to adapt to most environments. It has achieved this ubiquity despite also being the most abundant game species in North America; hunters typically bag over 20 million birds a year. Mourning Doves are a familiar species in city areas where they have a predilection for perching on telephone wires and devouring the seeds underneath backyard bird feeders. Look for Mourning Doves resting on the telephone wires along High Street and Long Lane.

IDENTIFICATION
Head and underparts are pale, sandy-brown. Back and wings darker grey-brown with bold black spots on the coverts and tertials. Tail is long and pointed.

VOICE
A mournful cooing, from which the species draws its name.

HOUSE SPARROW

Passer domesticus
L 6.3" (16 cm)
Year Round

The House Sparrow is a controversial bird. Depending on whom you ask, this species is either a brilliant opportunist or a destructive parasite. Like the city pigeon, this unassuming bird is surprisingly well-adapted to nesting in artificial human habitats (underneath eaves are a particular favorite). Since its introduction from the Old World into Brooklyn in 1851, the species has ridden the explosion of human development across the country. The success of the House Sparrow is so bound up with that of *homo sapiens* that it is rarely found somewhere where humans are not (which is to say they are found virtually everywhere in North America outside of Alaska). Unfortunately for many native species, this invasive defends its territory aggressively, often displacing other birds already sensitive to the impacts of anthropogenic forces. They have even been accused of evicting other birds by force from an active nest! This sparrow spends a lot of time on the ground, often congregated in noisy groups. Look for this species searching for crumbs around The Nest and along Lawn and Home Avenues.

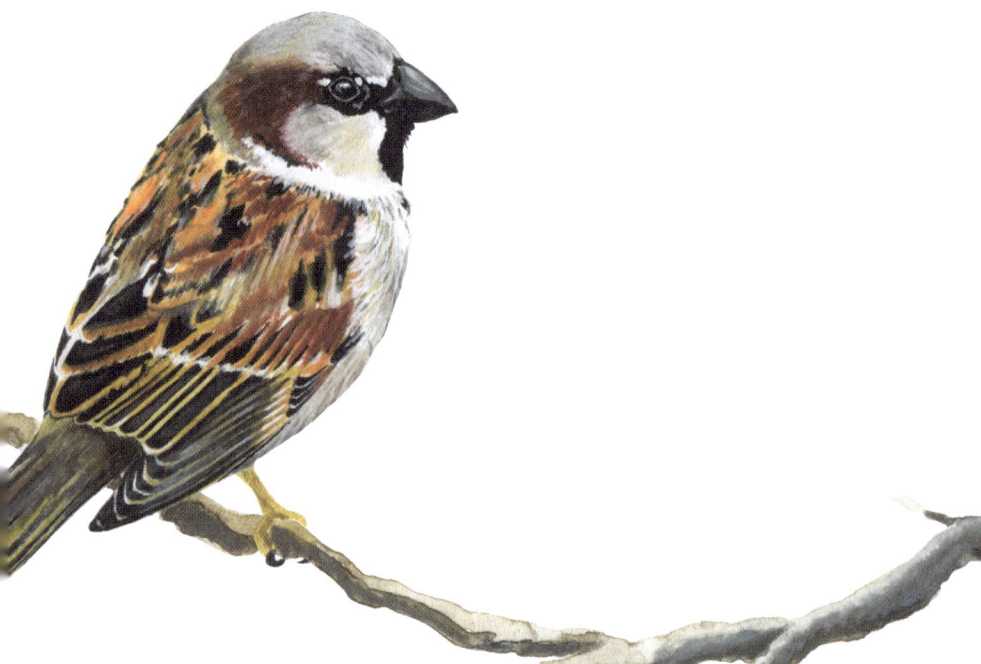

IDENTIFICATION

Male House Sparrows have gray heads, white cheeks, a black bib, and a rufous neck. Females are a plain buffy-brown overall.

VOICE

Call is a confident, incessant *chirrup.*

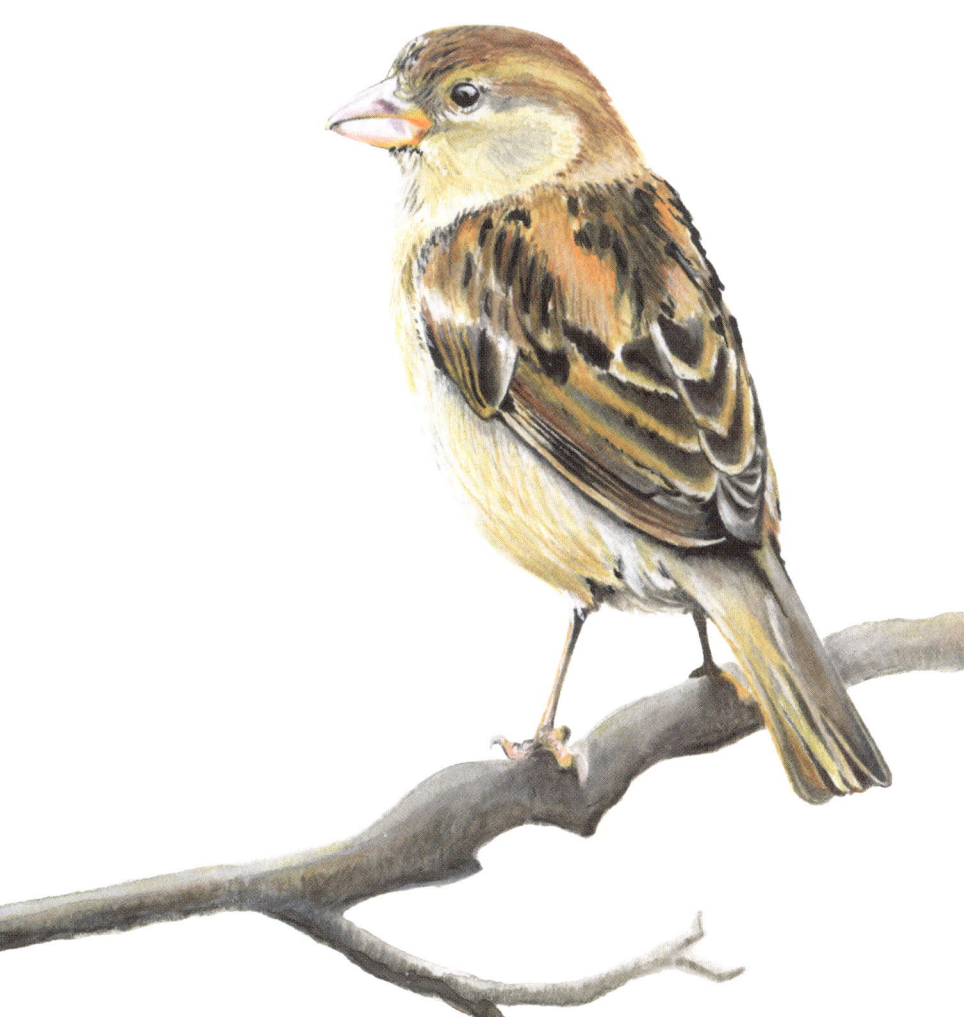

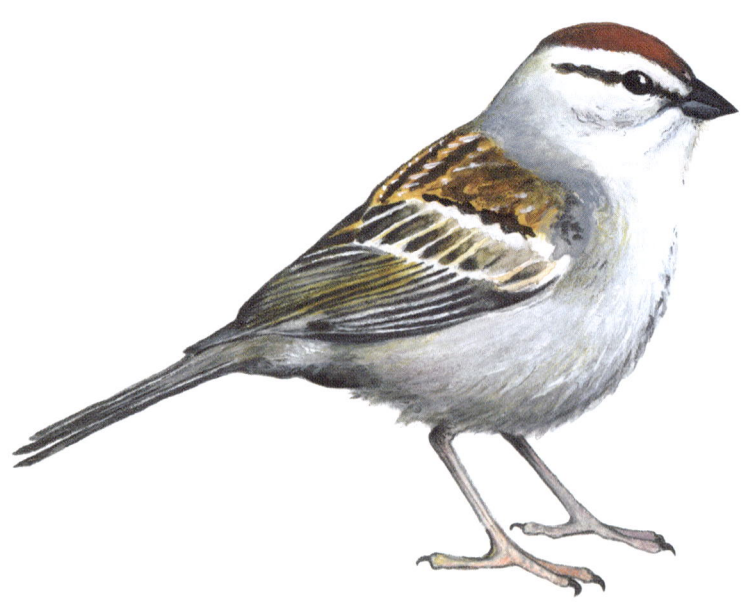

CHIPPING SPARROW

Spizella passerina
L 5.3" (13.5 cm)
April – October

There is a wispy quality to the Chipping Sparrow as if they might be carried away on the slightest breeze. Their presence is mouse-like and unimposing, frequently escaping the detection of even the most sensitive eye. But don't mistake this bird as less worthy of our attention: there is a rare satisfaction in slowing down to the subtle existence of creatures like these. Seeing the world through their eyes can be a humbling experience, a healthy reminder of the tenuous, miraculous existence of life. Even a relatively small animal like a squirrel, much less a human, must seem monstrous. Despite weighing only half an ounce, Chipping Sparrows prefer to sing from exposed perches, often belting their insect-like trill proudly from the tops of trees. Look for this bird foraging in small groups on the lawn in front of College Row and in the Butterfield's Courtyard.

IDENTIFICATION
Small and slender body. Crown is bright rusty-brown. Pale face with a black line through the eye. Underparts are pale. Wings and back are brown with dark streaks.

VOICE
A strong, metallic trill.

NORTHERN MOCKINGBIRD

Mimus polyglottus
L 9.75" (23 cm)
Year Round

The Northern Mockingbird continuously adds new songs to its repertoire throughout its life. One can learn a lot about the life history of a mockingbird from its playlist. "City" birds appropriate an urban soundtrack: car alarms, pedestrian crossing signals, reverse signals on big trucks, and sirens. "Country" birds at Wesleyan mimic the most vociferous birds around them. For instance, the mockingbird that has historically defended a territory at the Cross St. parking lot (the 'R' Lot) performs a convincing European Starling (imagine the sound of a tape deck on rewind). One would expect this because Starlings love to congregate on the radio tower across the street. This particular mockingbird also impersonates the Killdeer, a shorebird. On first thought, this might seem strange — a shorebird prefers aquatic habitats, difficult to find on Wesleyan's campus. Look across the street again, and there's your answer: Killdeer love to feed at the puddles that form on the Cross St. athletic fields. Listen for mockingbirds singing from conspicuous perches along Cross Street, outside Allbritton, and around the Admissions Office.

IDENTIFICATION
Grey-brown overall, paler on the breast and belly. Has long tail relative to body. In flight, white wing patches and white outer tail feathers flash evidently.

VOICE
Song highly variable. Often mimics other birds and human noises. Usually strings together sound bites of many impersonated sounds in rapid succession.

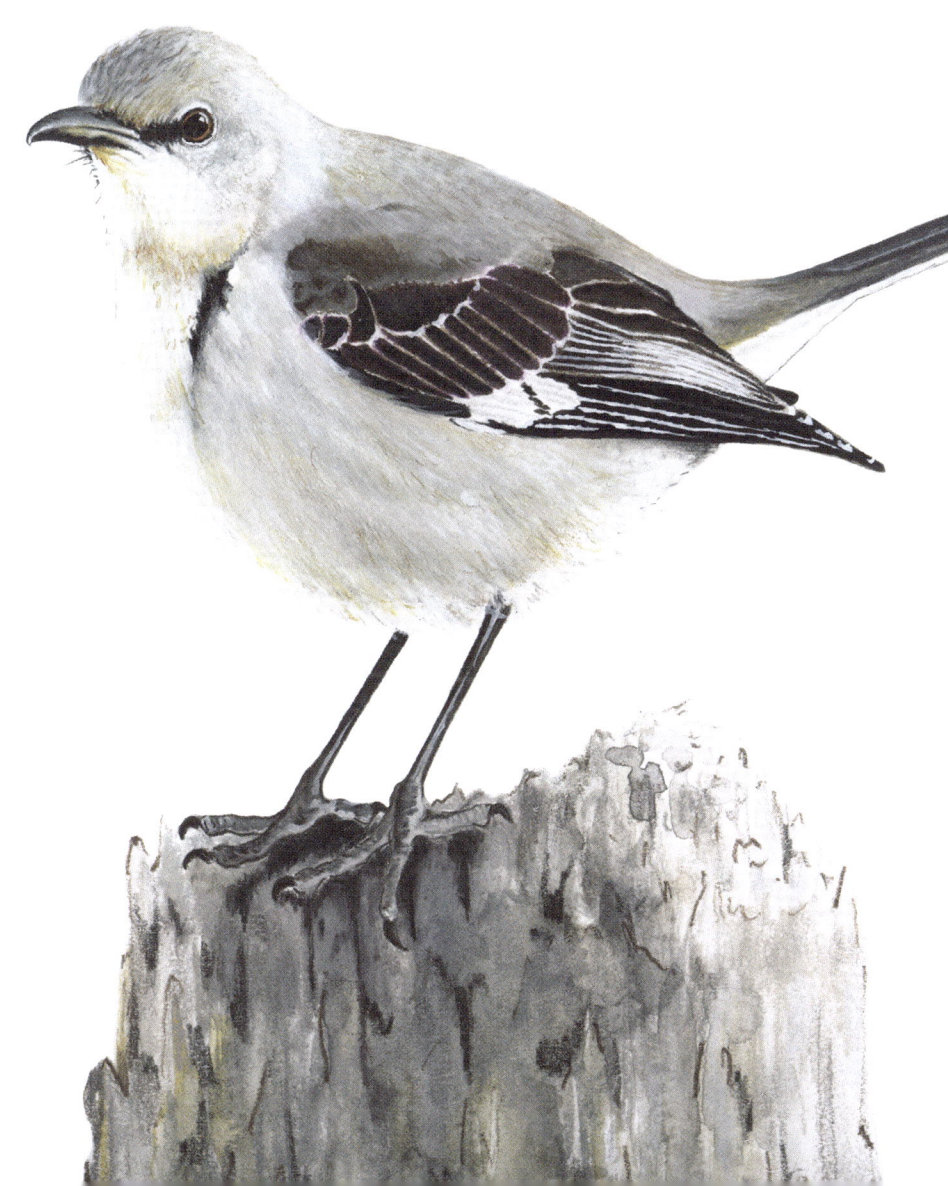

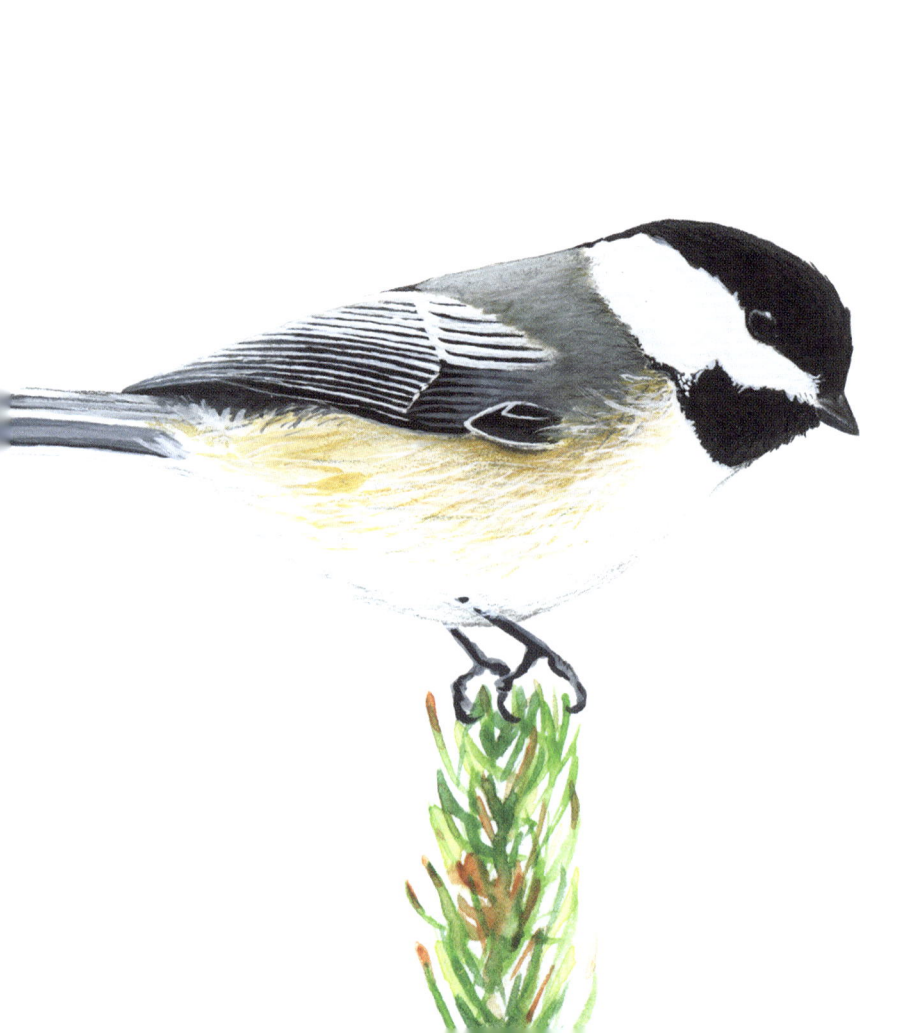

BLACK-CAPPED CHICKADEE

Parus atricapillus
L 5.25 " (13 cm)
Year Round

In the winter, when the "summer tourists" clear out, Chickadees band together into vociferous flocks that cruise the neighborhood in search of food and scandal. As in any small town, the gossip is incessant, and any experienced naturalist knows you can learn a lot by eavesdropping. For instance, Parids (chickadees and titmice) are known for a brash behavior called "mobbing," wherein everyone gets together and attempts to verbally harass a predator out of town. These bite-sized bundles of energy will confront just about anyone. Overhear this community alert and you can reliably locate an owl or hawk that might have otherwise remained inconspicuous. If you run into a chickadee flock out of breeding season look for the odd bird out — there usually is one — as it's prudent for a migratory bird to fall in with this crowd. They know the good eats. Look for chickadees in the mid-canopy of a variety of trees on campus.

IDENTIFICATION
Head pattern is diagnostic: both male and female have a black cap, strong white cheeks, and a black bib. Back is grey. Their strong feet allow them to forage opportunistically, often hanging upside down to get a better angle on a tasty morsel.

VOICE
Says its name, a wheezy *chick-a-dee-dee-dee*. Song is a two-note clear, whistled *fee-bee* or three-note *fee-bee-ee*, the first note higher in pitch.

AMERICAN ROBIN
Turdus migratorius
L 10" (25 cm)
Year Round

Partial to sod, Robins navigate the front lawn at a unique run-and-stop tempo. Between their short scurries, they freeze and cock their head to the side. Close observation of this behavior might imply that these birds have acutely sensitive ears, as if straining to hear the earthworms wriggling under the dirt. In actuality, the birds are relying on their eyesight. Robins are commonly associated with the arrival of spring, but it is ironically during the winter months that robins are present on campus in their greatest density. The berry crop of many common ornamental trees and shrubs can support large numbers of robins through to the spring. Look for flocks feasting on the fruiting dogwoods along Church St. during the winter months.

IDENTIFICATION
Head is black or dark grey with white eye arcs. Bill is yellow. Throat streaked black and white. Underparts vary: males have richer red chest and belly, females are salmon-colored. Upperparts grey-brown; tail blackish. Posture is often erect with bill tipped upward.

VOICE
Song is a combination of clear, whistled phrases spaced out by short pauses: *cheerily cheery cheerily cheery.*

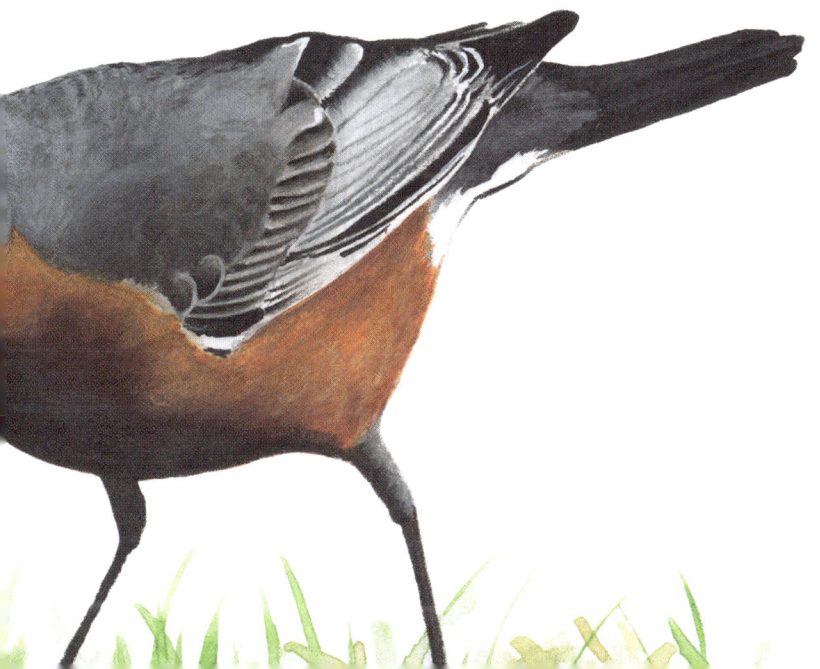

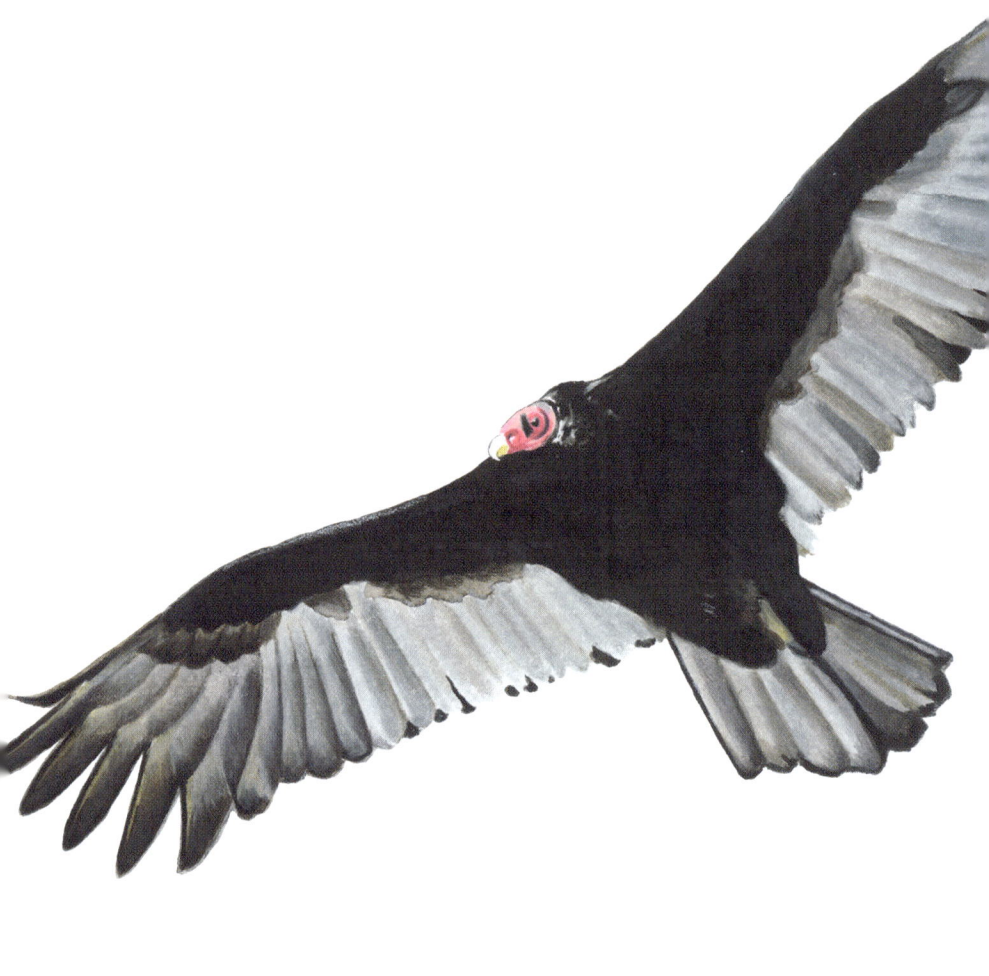

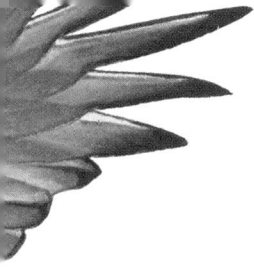

TURKEY VULTURE
Cathartes aura
L 27" WS 69"
Absent in winter

Rarely descending on campus grounds, the Turkey Vulture is one of the largest birds typically seen soaring over campus. Vultures are nature's garbage collectors: consumers of carrion, they have an excellent sense of smell, purportedly keen enough to detect road kill on Washington St. all the way from the Butterfields. Wesleyan sits on a hill and vultures enjoy the free ride created from the thermals rising off its incline. They often seem to be inspecting students on Foss for signs of life as they spiral lazily overhead. Seen from below, the contrasting two-toned wings aid in differentiation from the closely-related Black Vulture, which also visits campus. Like all vultures, the Turkey Vulture has a small un-feathered head, pink in this case, which aids in sanitation. Guts are a messy business – like a beard, feathers around the face would quickly gather unwanted crumbs. Don't rely on their naked head as a field mark, as the head is often imperceptible to the unaided eye at its preferred altitudes. Look for these gargoyles riding thermals over Foss Hill.

IDENTIFICATION
Black overall with a bald pink head and strongly hooked bill. Most reliable field mark is diagnostic two-toned underwing pattern, where the entire trailing edge of the wing is whiter than the leading edge. The Black Vulture, in contrast, has pale white only at the fingertips.

VOICE
Generally silent in the field.

ACKNOWLEDGEMENTS

To appropriately recognize all those who have shaped and inspired the creation of this book it is necessary to start at the very beginning.

Thank you first and foremost to Anne Whaling and Christopher James. I cannot thank you enough for your patience and dedication as parents and providing me with the time and encouragement to chase my dreams.

Rich Stallcup: shaman, teacher, sage. You took me under your wing when I was 10 years old and my life changed forever. You will be sorely missed.

Heartfelt appreciation goes out to all my mentors who nurtured my interest in birds from a young age. There are too many to name here. A deep bow to each and all.

A huge thank you to all my talented friends and colleagues who assisted in the production of this field guide. You, sir Alec Harris, are a fearless leader and patient editor. Thank you also to Alex Ginsberg, Julia Randall, Laura Grey and Hannah Cressy for technical help with design and editing. Last but not least a big shoutout is due to all the authors and editors of Stethoscope 2014. It has been a pleasure working alongside you.

Special thanks to the generous financial support of those that made this book possible, including:

The COLLEGE OF THE ENVIRONMENT, with special thanks to Barry Chernoff

The WESLEYAN WRITING PROGRAM

The WESLEYAN GREEN FUND was established in the Spring of 2010 with the support of the student body, the Wesleyan Student Assembly, and the Board of Trustees. The Green Fund projects are chosen for funding based on their ability to increase the University's use of renewable energy sources, decrease the University's carbon footprint, or decrease waste. The Fund exists to spur creativity, innovation, and collaboration within the Wesleyan student body, faculty, and staff, to empower green initiatives on campus.

ABOUT THE AUTHOR

Oliver James was born in Berkeley, CA in 1991. He started watching birds avidly at age 5 and never turned back. Since then, he has competed in national birding tournaments, worked as a birding tour guide, and joined ornithological research teams in Peru and Alaska. He graduated from Wesleyan University in 2014 with a degree in Biology and Environmental Studies.

INFORMATION ABOUT THE ORIGINAL STETHOSCOPE EDITION

This book was part of the STETHOSCOPE PRESS 2013–2014 Series. Each book was printed in an edition of 300.

STETHOSCOPE PRESS publishes individual books by individual student authors. We pair each writer with a personal editor with whom to work on their projects. Our designers then guide the authors and editors to give the books an appealing physical form. We value the collaboration between writer, editor, and designer, and we believe in the importance of long-form writing.

This book was funded by Wesleyan's Student Budgetary Committee, Wesleyan's Writing Program, The Wesleyan Green Fund and The College of the Environment.

Thanks to Davy Knittle '11 for creating STETHOSCOPE PRESS.

Text set in Archer.

BOOKS IN THE SERIES:
A Field Guide to the Birds of Wesleyan by Oliver James
Cisco by Amy Mattox
Cartwheel Infinite by Ananya Menon
Our Happy Throng by Hailey Sowden
On Interconnectivity... by Sean Winnik

HEAD EDITOR: Alec Harris

DESIGNER: Alex Ginsberg

SERIES EDITORS: Adam Bresgi, Julia Conrad, Anna Guth, Joshua Krugman, Kayla Stoler